COLLECTION
My Dog & friends
BOOKS

Encouraging critical thinking in children contributes to their personal growth and social progress. Thanks to all of those who are committed to this work.

FRIDA, A BARK OF HOPE

© 2023 Written by Julia Pérez Villegas
© 2023 Illustrated by Alessandra Canu

Project management: Sergio de la Varga Robles
Published by My Dog & friends Books
www.mydogandfriendsbooks.com

Translated by Rebecca James
Designed by Silvina Eduardo

ISBN: 9798865717560
First edition: July 2023

For 5-year-olds and above

All rights reserved

FRIDA

A bark of hope

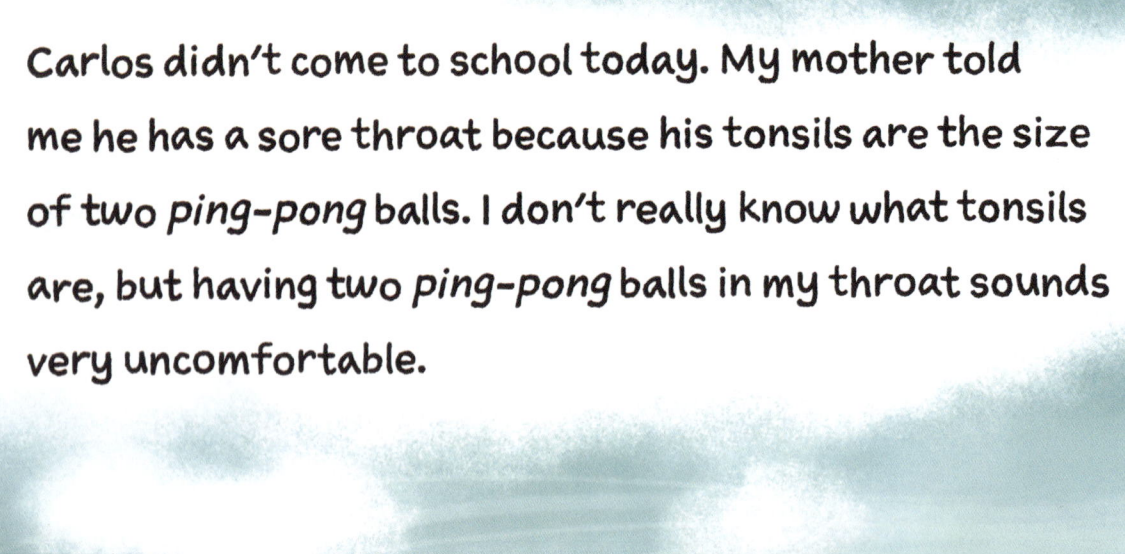

Carlos didn't come to school today. My mother told me he has a sore throat because his tonsils are the size of two *ping-pong* balls. I don't really know what tonsils are, but having two *ping-pong* balls in my throat sounds very uncomfortable.

Since I'm his best friend, I'm also in charge of filling him in on everything we've done. Including homework: how boring, right? I'd normally think so, but this morning turned out to be more interesting than I expected it to be when the alarm clock went off.

As soon as I got home, I picked up the phone and called him.

When Carlos answered, in a voice so hoarse he sounded like he was fifty or a hundred years old, I asked him:

— Have you ever heard of Frida?

— Frida Kahlo, the painter? Of course I know her! My mother's a huge fan, answered Carlos, clearing his throat between words.

— No, not that Frida. Frida, the rescue dog. Come on, grab an orange juice or a mint, or both, and I'll tell you what happened in class today...

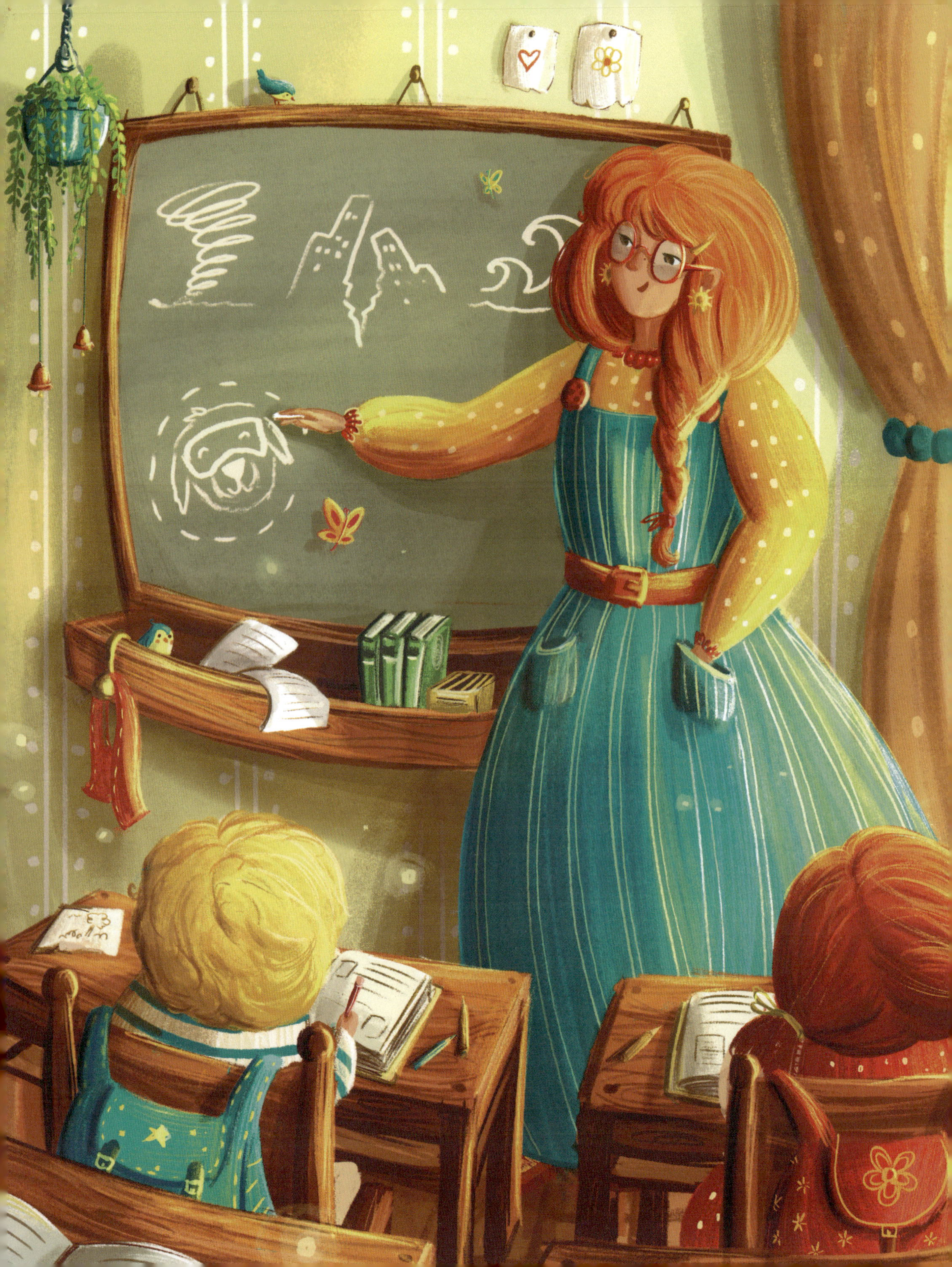

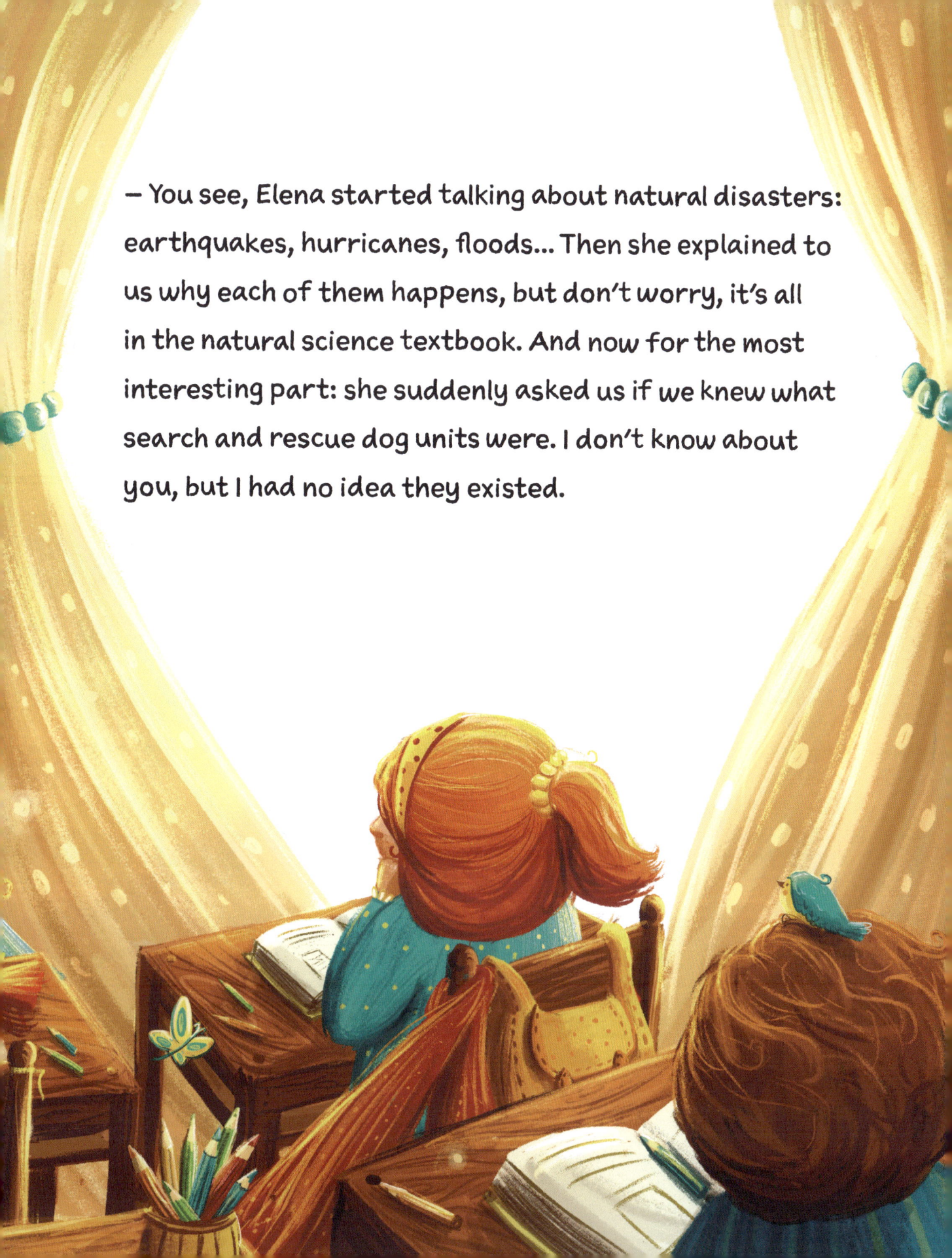

— You see, Elena started talking about natural disasters: earthquakes, hurricanes, floods... Then she explained to us why each of them happens, but don't worry, it's all in the natural science textbook. And now for the most interesting part: she suddenly asked us if we knew what search and rescue dog units were. I don't know about you, but I had no idea they existed.

— Neither did I, said Carlos very quietly.

— Well, it turns out that when earthquakes happen, buildings collapse, you know, and people get trapped in the rubble. Then the firemen, the police and other people come and help. Rescue dogs are also brought in, as they can get into tricky places and have a better sense of smell than humans.

So they know where people are buried and bark for rescue. These dogs can save your life.

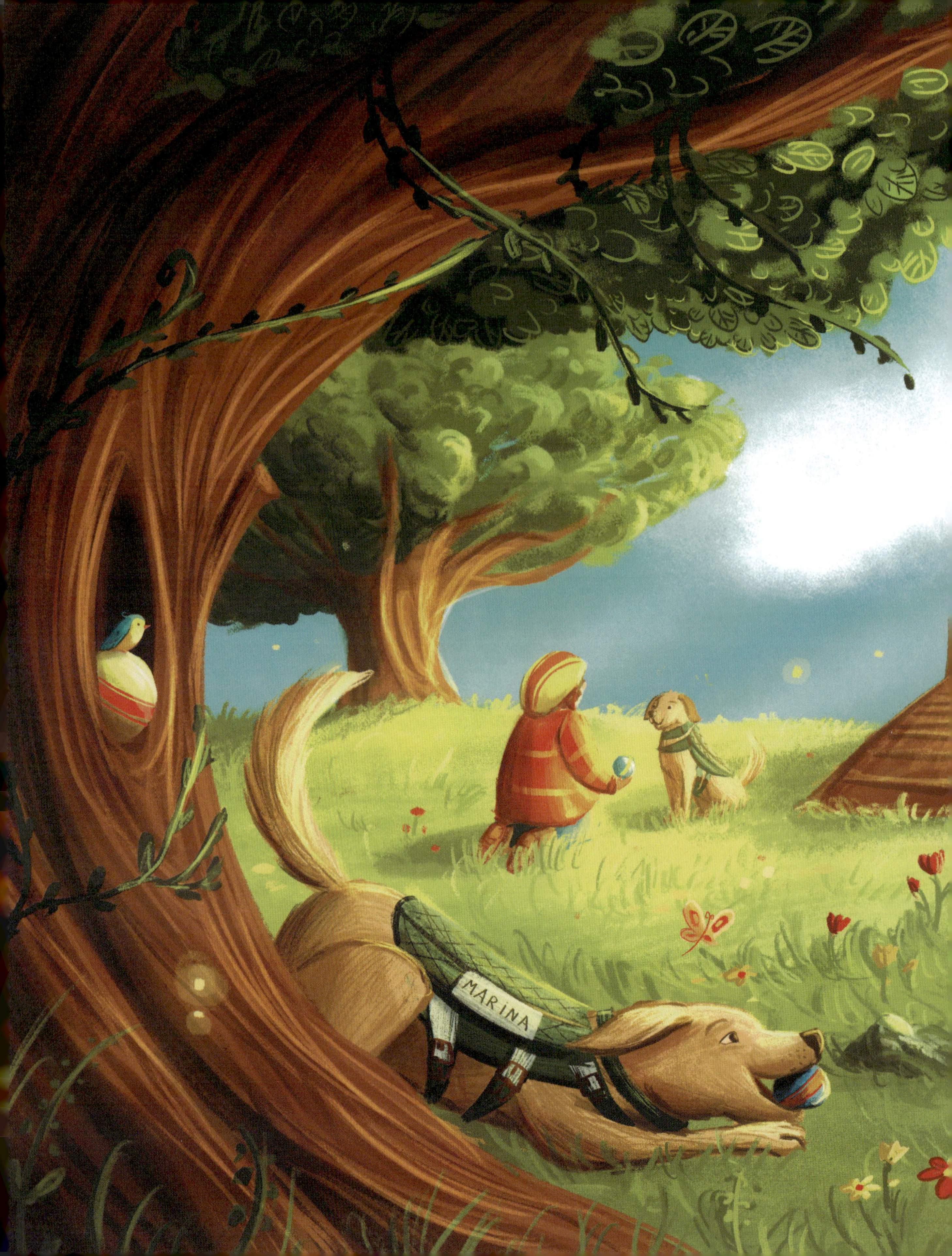
MARINA

— Unbelievable! But how do they learn to look for people? — asked Carlos, who sounded more and more interested in the story.

— Let me tell you: their trainers hide their favourite toys for them to find. They also distract them with fire, noises and so on so that they get used to them and don't get lost or scared when they're searching. It takes them a whole year before they are ready to help out.

— Elena gave us the example of Frida the dog. She was born in a Mexican Navy rescue dog school. She joined the canine unit when she was only six months old, and there she started training with other dogs, and was ready after only eight months! But then she kept on training every day, until she retired, just like my grandparents retired.

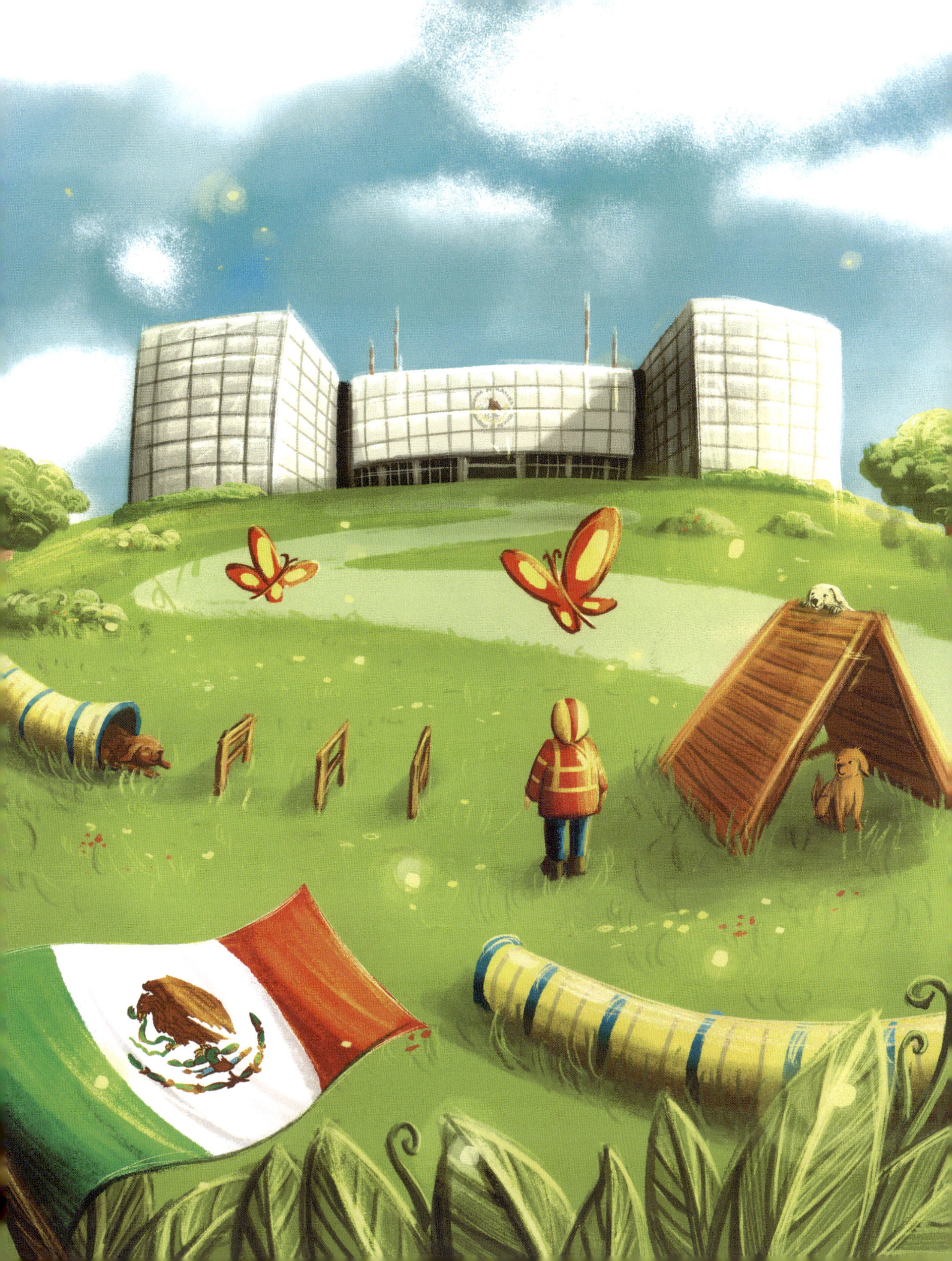

— We saw a video of how she trained: first a person would grab Frida's favourite toy, run away and lie down on the floor for the dog to find it. All the while, Frida sat still, very quietly, next to her trainer. I tell you, if it had been my dog Harry, he would have run for his toy. When she was given the command, the dog, who had seen where the other man had laid down, ran towards him, and when she reached his side she barked to warn him. He would then give her her toy and she would be overjoyed. Then they made it even more difficult: the man would hide again with Frida's toy, but this time without her seeing him, and the dog would find him by following his scent. Frida thoroughly enjoyed that game.

— And did they give her a uniform like the firemen's? — Carlos asked.

— Yes, a special tailor-made one. Her trainer said in the video that in just two days she had got used to wearing it. It had a safety harness and a collar that said "Marina", safety goggles and little neoprene boots that prevented her from getting burnt, electrocuted or hurt when walking through the rubble. It looked great on her, but more importantly, she was well protected.

FRIDA

— How funny, and did she only have one trainer? — Carlos interrupted me.

— Good question! Yes, she only had one trainer and, together they formed a "canine binomial", which, although it sounds like mathematics, Elena explained to us is the team made up of the dog and its trainer. Israel is the person who trained Frida. He loved her very much, and she loved him, and I saw how she looked at him in the videos and the licks she gave him whenever he was distracted. The affection and trust between the two of them were very important, to make sure they worked well as a team whenever they had to rush out and help.

— And did she manage to rescue anyone? — Carlos asked.

— Of course she did! Wait, I'm going to get my notebook, I wrote it all down so I didn't forget, because I couldn't believe it: Frida found twelve people alive and forty-three dead following various earthquakes and disasters in Haiti, Ecuador and Mexico. That's a total of fifty-five bodies located — which is a lot! Israel said she could smell people eight to ten metres beneath the rubble. Do you know how much that is? More than two giraffes on top of each other.

— Wow, I'm speechless, and not because of my sore throat, whispered Carlos.

— Yeah, the same thing happened to me in class, and I normally can't even keep my mouth shut under water! But I got goosebumps when I thought of the people who were trapped and heard Frida barking. Surely at that moment they knew they had been found and could be rescued. Frida's bark gave them hope.

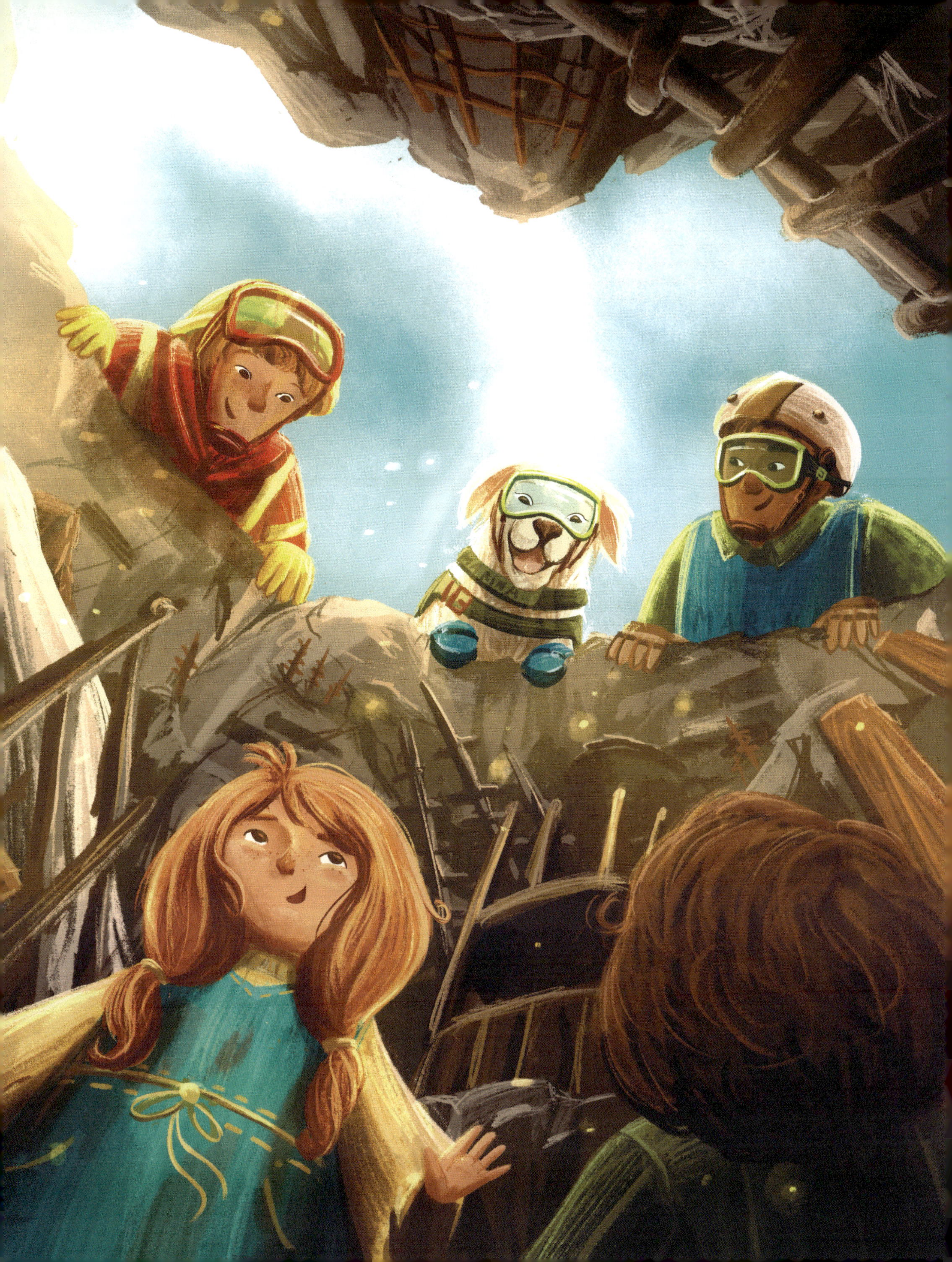

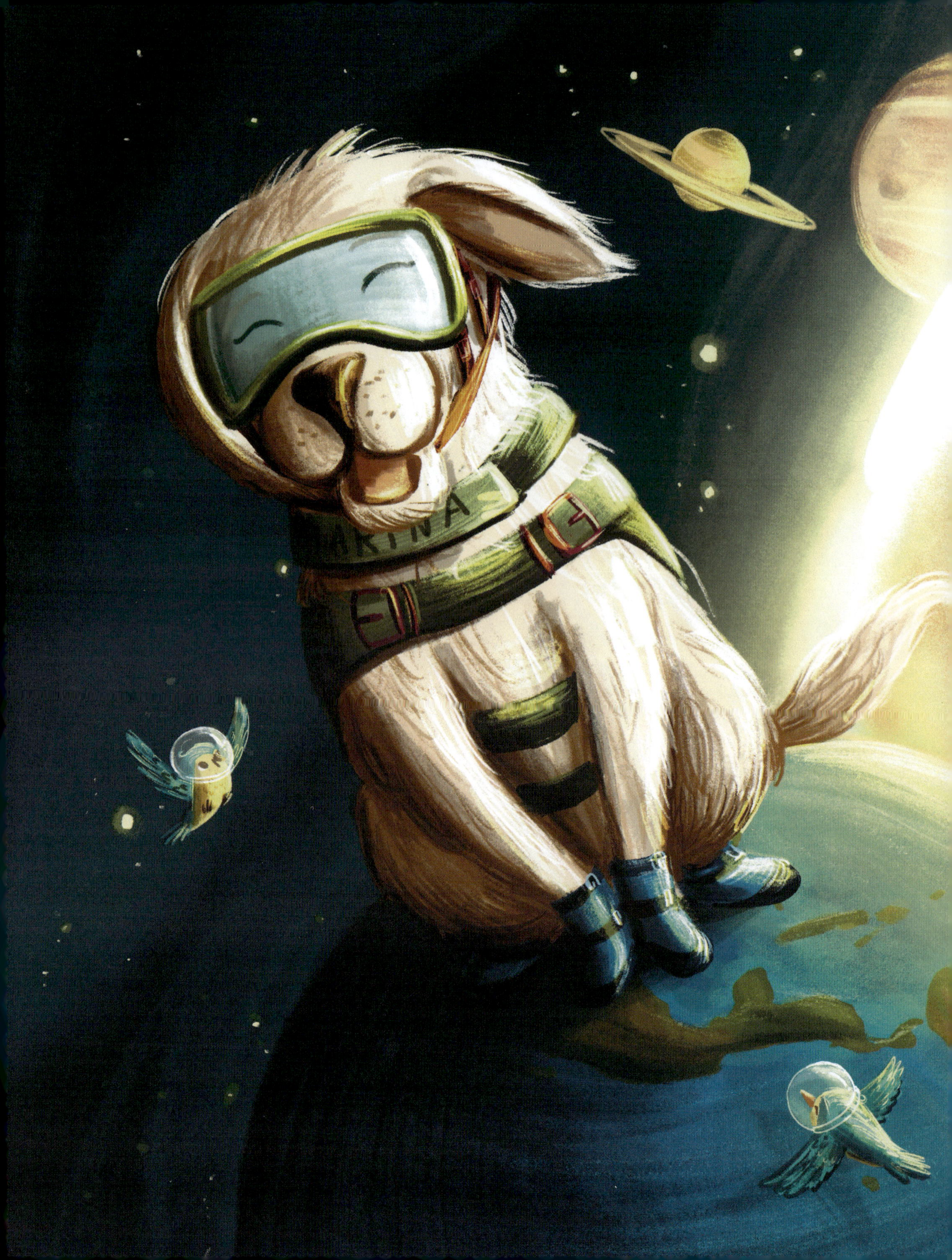

— Because she helped so many people, she became a heroine. In Mexico they were very proud of her and the whole country admired her. And not only in Mexico: Frida was famous even in Japan! In fact, they called her Marina there, because they got confused with the letters on her uniform and thought it was her name.

— They got it all wrong! How long did she work for the canine unit? — he asked.

— Over ten years! Until 2019, and she retired on International Rescuer Day. They gave her a big retirement party. Some very important people thanked her and said very nice things about her. Then Frida went up on the stage with her uniform and Israel took it off with great affection, and, as a prize, they gave her a ball, which was one of her favourite toys.

— And then what happened to Frida? — Carlos asked.

— She stayed in the centre where she had lived until then, and rested, which she deserved. Although she no longer trained, she supported the young dogs as they did, because, without a doubt, Frida was a great teacher.

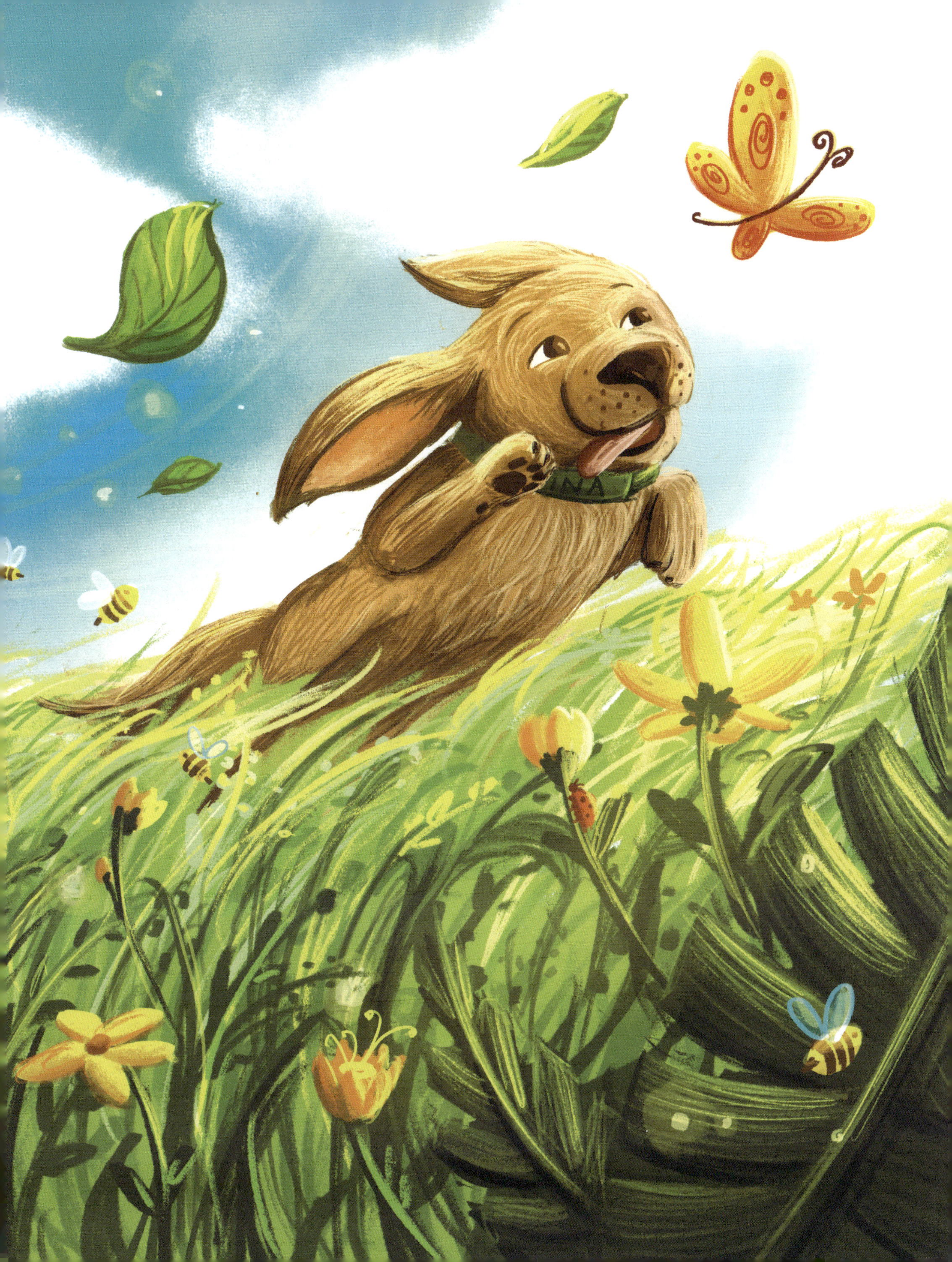
INA

ENTRADA   ENTRADA

FRIDA

– When Frida was thirteen, they made her a bronze statue! That's how much they loved her in Mexico. She and her trainer were there when they unveiled the statue and again everyone said how noble, generous and good she was. I'm sure that on the way back Israel shed a tear or two, and Frida gave a lick or two.

— Elena told us that Frida died a few months later. Thirteen years is a long time for a dog as big as Frida. I couldn't help but feel a little sad. In Mexico people really mourned for her, but her bark of hope will always live on in all the people she helped so much.

— Thank you, Marta. Thank you, Frida, said Carlos, swallowing, either because of the *ping-pong* balls or the emotion.

— You're welcome, Carlos. I hope you get well soon. I'll call you tomorrow.

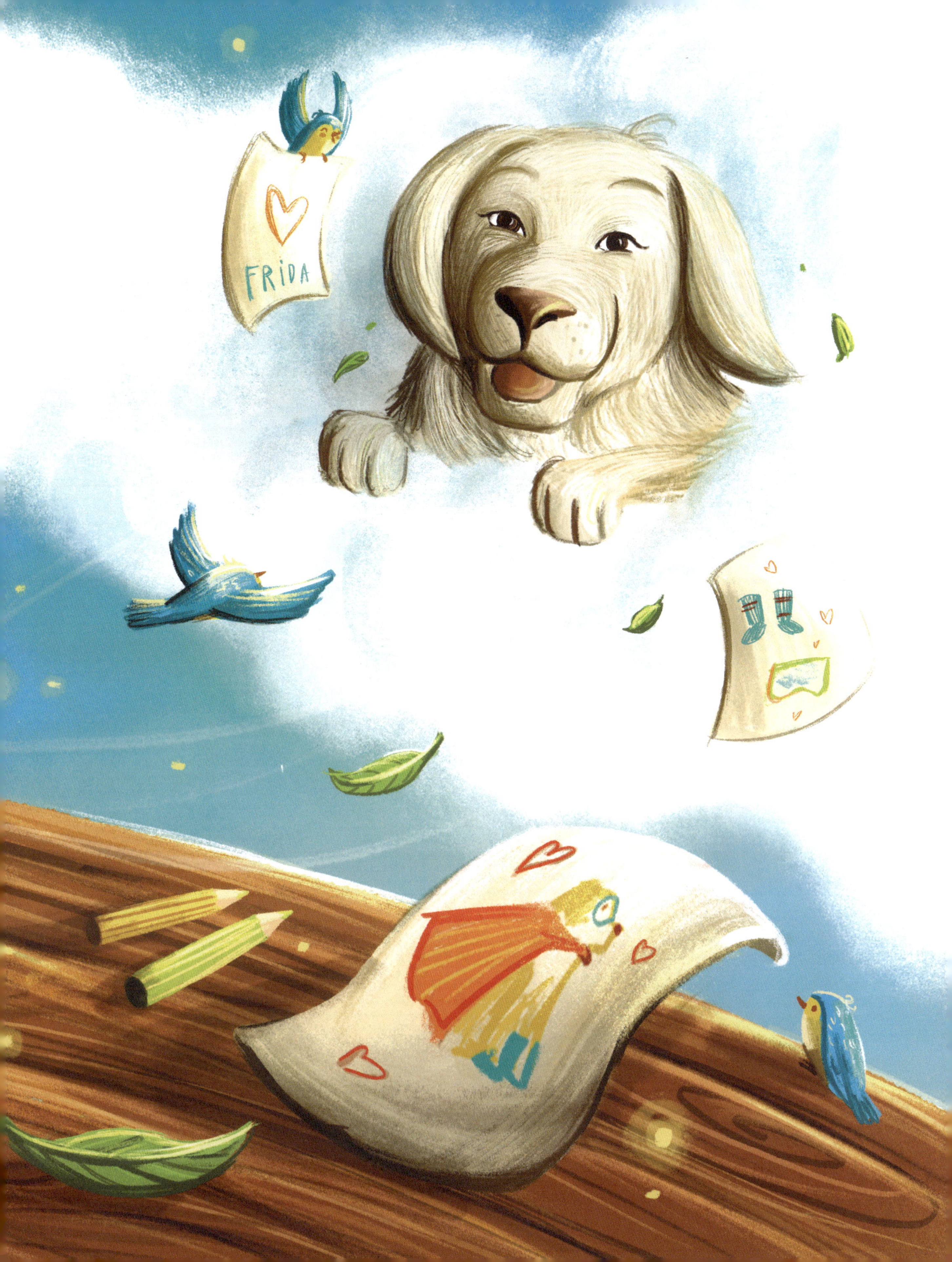
FRIDA

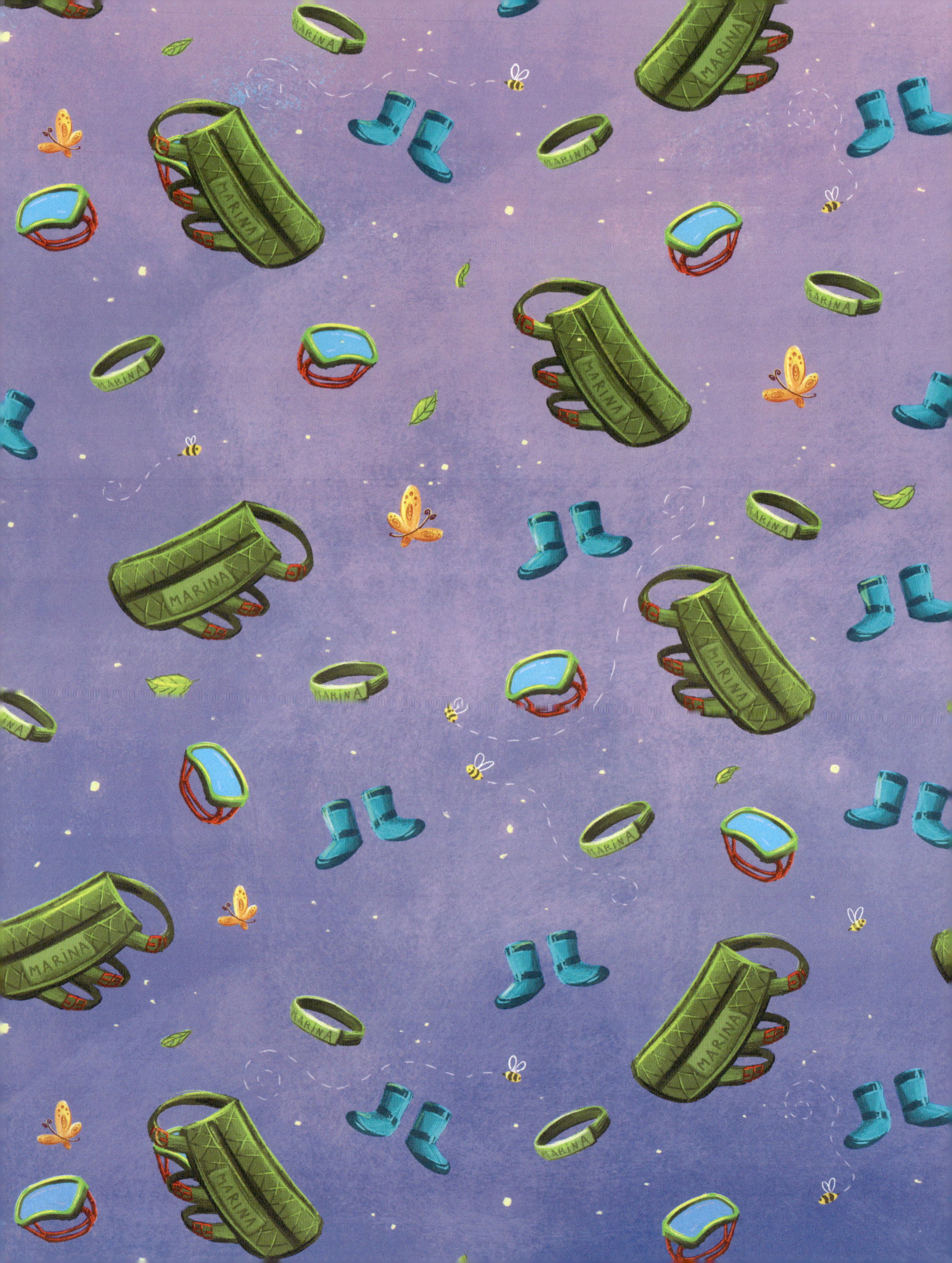
MARINA